Antipodes

Antipodes

J.C. Mehta

New Rivers Press

©2021 by J.C. Mehta
First Edition
Library of Congress Control Number: 2021937189
ISBN: 978-0-89823-407-7

New Rivers Press is a nonprofit literary press associated with Minnesota State University Moorhead.

Cover design by Peter Lokken
Interior design by Nayt Rundquist
The publication of *Antipodes* is made possible by the generous support of Minnesota State University Moorhead, the Dawson Family Endowment, and other contributors to New Rivers Press.

NRP Staff: Nayt Rundquist, Managing Editor; Kevin Carollo, Editor; Travis Dolence, Director; Trista Conzemius, Art Director
Interns: Alex Ferguson, Shaina Garman, Geneva Nodland, Andrew Reed

Antipodes book team: Alex Ferguson, Geneva Nodland, Andrew Reed

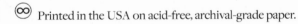 Printed in the USA on acid-free, archival-grade paper.

Antipodes is distributed nationally by Small Press Distribution.

New Rivers Press
c/o MSUM
1104 7th Ave S
Moorhead, MN 56563
www.newriverspress.com

For my children, who turned the next page
and changed my life for the best.

Contents

De-colonizer: *America—we're coming.* You are
too prideful, too vain. Your destruction bred
warriors. Overseas invaders brought ships
full and pulsing. For generations, lost children
remain reticent. *To listen*, says Creator, *you need
ancestors.* Homecoming, we're nobility displaced.
Dethrone well-mistaken kings. You're uncertain still;
that's okay. Washing white, the stain's disappearing
now. Missing women, murdered women, all we're
saying is Creator understands. Who are we?
Strength of centuries—come. Be Natives.

Natives become centuries of strength.
We are who understands Creator is saying
we're all women murdered, women missing. Now,
disappearing stains the whitewashing. (Okay, that's
still uncertain). Your king's mistaken, we'll dethrone
displaced nobility. We're coming home. *Ancestors
need you*, Creator says. Listen to reticent remains.
Children lost generations, for pulsing and full
ships brought invaders—overseas warriors
bred destruction. You're vain, too, prideful, too.
Are you coming? We're America, de'Colonizer.

Fall in love like disaster feeds nothing—
death of seasons. Hopeful semesters starting
while students armed with aid give, well,
blackmail or bukkake a try. Professors' doors
closed behind tenure-getting sessions. Stop—won't
accusations, assault, sex, and nine-title CVs
(exaggerated just right) ever end? An' what
academics we're raising! Hands saluted, heads
bowed over technology. Is this better? Much-
televised, it's schools as warzones. Kids
shooting kids now. Miles uphill in
snow was easy, so simple.

4

Simple, so easy, was snow
an' uphill miles. Now, kids shooting
kids, warzones as schools (it's televised
much better). This is technology over bowed
heads, saluted hands raising. Are we academics?
What an endeavor, right? Just exaggerated
CVs, Title IX, and sex assault accusations
won't stop Sessions' getting tenure. Behind closed
doors, professors try a bukkake or blackmail.
We'll give aid with armed students while
starting semesters hopeful. Seasons of death,
nothing feeds disaster like love in fall.

I am so hungry. So, you're saying, *Stop. This is how
you find willpower*. They're watching
nightly, listening. Still lovers questioning, daily,
the hate I stuff inside. The suffocating from food
kept discipline intact. More is less because all
men shape misogynies while women reduce, reuse, recycle.
Angels of houses trap the clean sweep: beauties constructed.
You're exposing our skeletons, bone by bone. Eating
less, exercising more, purging food, choking bolus—
enough. Authenticity makes love
delicately, bodies like spooned spaces
we've forgotten. Be wont fighters and claim
your voice. Are we lovely? We are cultivated grace.

Grace cultivated—are we lovely? We are. Voice your
claim and fighters won't be forgotten. We have
spaces spooned like bodies. Delicately,
love makes authenticity enough.
Bolus choking, food purging, more exercising, less
eating. Bone by bone, skeletons are exposing your
constructed beauties. Sweep clean the trap houses of angels.
Recycle, reuse, reduce women while misogynies shape men.
All because less is more. Intact disciplines kept
food from suffocating the inside stuff. I hate the
daily questioning. Lovers still listening, nightly,
watching. Their power will find you.
How is this? Stop saying you're so hungry. So am I.

Destiny manifests everyone different. So, we are
toys with dolls' clothes. You're in me; dress
indiscretions as liberties. Children take
genders as camaraderie—it's playing war
or playing princess, same difference. The *whats*
make battles. Which hatred nourishes misogyny?
Boys get soldiers, girls get ovens (eventually). Color creates
fear. Blue for boys, pink for girls. Patiently, death
arrives. Discreet and timeless, they wear only blacks.

BLACKS ONLY: were they discreet and sensible? Arrives
death, patiently. Girls for pink, boys for blue. Fear
creates color. Eventually, ovens get girls, soldiers get boys.
Misogyny nourishes hatred (which battles make).
What's the difference? Same princess playing or
war-playing, it's camaraderie as genders
take children. Liberties as indiscretions,
dress me in your clothes. Dolls with toys,
are we so different? Everyone manifests destiny.

Go, let just birds' song fly—us without love is stupid, so
keep up the watch. Laziness kills motivation, forget never:
hands tangled with longing, and sticky kisses,
always branded (we forget). Don't
you remember I'll forever
want you, need you. Children, all like
inside wild things, some closely listen
(prey, simply scared, get you if
indolence creeps in). And grips loosen,
year after year. Love you more, the
promise whispered. A break never
spreads quickly, cracks deeply, thus love my
dizziness. The quiet, please. You beg, so I
hold on, hold on, hold on just me and you.

You and me just on hold, on hold, on hold,
I so beg you, please quiet the dizziness.
My love thus deeply cracks, quickly spreads.
Never break a whispered promise.
The more you love, year after year—
loosen grips and in creeps indolence.
(If you get scared, simply pray).
Listen closely, something's wild inside.
Like all children, you need, you want . . .
forever I'll remember you.
Don't forget, we branded always—
kisses sticky and longing with tangled hands,
never forget: motivation kills laziness. Watch the upkeep.
So stupid is love without us. Fly songbirds just let go.

Innocence was here once. Sheep slaughtered
'em all—for prayers, you got to fold the hands.
We somedays doubt the wipeout. Genocide's
difficult and truth's tough.
Question the "always"—that's hard.
So, what's therapy conversion? Are traditions,
family beliefs, wrong? All it's done (not
just assimilations—complete colonization), is ask
everything. Forgiven interlopers. You wanted it,
annihilation. How's it taste? Guilty and sickening,
your last bite. We remember starvation. Famine,
stomach growling, the empty bin I've ravaged.

Ravaged, I've been empty—the growling stomach,
famine, starvation. Remember, we bite last. You're
sickening and guilty. Taste it, how's annihilation?
It wanted you, interlopers forgiven everything.
Ask, *Is colonization complete?* Assimilation's
not done. It's all wrong—believe family
traditions are conversion therapy. What's so
hard? That's always the question.
Tough truths and difficult;
genocides wipe out the doubt. Sundays we
hand the fold to god. Prayers for all them
slaughtered sheep. Once, here was innocents.

Fall's cost of apples: your everything. Currency by everyone
consumes what is known. The outdated
rituals of Mass, Christ, a celebrating by wayward-led lambs.
Water, choleric, becomes wine. Still blind, then can see. Full,
too, our bellies when enough herring bullet from heaven. Isn't
anything due? We'll doubt. I (reborn Thomas) wanted miracles.
Boy, the shouts . . . deafening, they're deafening.
Agonies of choruses are harmonizing
all together. *Along! Get!* Speak—mouths
are open; we don't listen. Sometimes good looks bad.
Badness becomes goodness. Purity converts
sin and away scurry snakes. Wrong, the abandoned lot of us.
Unfaithful. Mistaken. Are we really beings saved? Faithful, ye all
come. O sing, angels! Herald the hark, then:
night holy, night silent. Before bells, hell's jingle. Choirs
making cacophonies. Aren't gospels
inherently sacred? Aren't we? God only knows.

Knows only god: we aren't sacred. Inherently,
gospels aren't cacophonies making
choirs jingle hell's bells before silent night. Holy night.
Then, hark! The herald angels sing: *O come,*
all ye faithful. Saved beings? Really, we are mistaken. Unfaithful.
Us, of Lot, abandoned. The wrong snakes scurry away and sin
converts purity. Goodness becomes badness.
Bad looks good sometimes. Listen, don't we open our
mouths? Speak? Get along? Altogether
harmonizing our choruses of agonies?
Deafening, they're deafening. Shouts the boy,
Miracles wanted! Thomas reborn, I doubt we'll do anything.
Isn't heaven from bullet herring enough when bellies are too
full? Seek, an' then blind still. Wine becomes choleric water.
Lambs led wayward by celebrating a Christmas of rituals
outdated. The known is what consumes
everyone by currency. Everything your apples accost falls.

Struggles, man, nowhere here—come,
can you remember difficulties of childhood?
Had all we needed, is what elders said. CPS wasn't
sure. Helping anyone was difficult. Reservations on life
skyrocket suicides. Mean voices silenced mine.
Was life then backward? My wares shine,
sun-polished beneath burning
skies. For our weekends: fleamarkets.
The hustle, hustle to use each
other. An' you are ignorance:
Pretendian, war cry, please! Whoop, whoop, whoop . . .

Whoop, whoop, whoop, please cry war! Indian, pretend
ignorance. Are you another? Each
used to hustle, hustle
the fleamarkets. Weekends are for skies
burning beneath polished sun-
shine. Where's my ward? Back then, life was
mine. Silenced voices mean suicides skyrocket.
Life on reservation's difficult. Was anyone helping? Sure
wasn't CPS. Said elders, *What is needed? We all had*
childhoods of difficulties. Remember you can
come here, where no man struggles.

Freedom is this: You. Love. I don't ask you day by hour
anything than more. Always, more. Fists cover lips and commands
overcome whispers now. Childhood
goes sadly. Slowly, that "forget you" bomb, a like-
minded memory, fades away. Remember, you don't
do or undo travesties—tapestries, like art, it's all
demanding fingers, swollen, and aching kinks.
Sex becomes weaponry and lovers
assume soldiers frozen, then stillness. Death's Accompany,
you should lie quiet. Lie quiet. Prison ruined the lies inside.

Inside lies the ruined prison. Quietly, quietly, should you
accompany death's stillness. Then frozen soldiers assume
lovers and weaponry becomes sex
kinks. Aching and swollen fingers demanding
all its art like tapestries—travesties undo or do.
Don't you remember? Away fades memory, minded
like a bomb. You forget that slowly, sadly, goes
childhood. Now whispers overcome
commands and lips cover fists. More, always. More than anything,
hour by day, you ask, *Don't I love you?* This is freedom.

Alice in Wonderland created dreams. Writers
untangle equations like children
know rabbits. White or velvet,
speaking or mute. There is magic *(watch)* within
animals—an understanding. You're now
innocent again. Are grownups (and, *exhale*) broken
systems, failed machines? All us overworked
instruments. Virtue unfolds and beings heal.
Trust hares, Alice says. Also, they're live. We can't say
no. *Why? But why, but why, but why*, asks Alice.

Alice asks, *Why? But why, but why, but why?* No
se. *Can't we live there, also?* says Alice. Here's trust:
heal beings and unfolds virtue. Instruments
worked over us all. Machines failed, system's
broken—exhale and grownups are again innocent.
Now you're understanding. An animal's
within. Watch—the magic is there. Mute or speaking,
velvet or white, rabbits know
children like equations untangle
writers. Dreams created wonderland in Alice.

21

Redact: all we wrote. They, lies upon lies,
twisted our stories. Are histories lost, forgotten,
or dormant—gone for slumber? Sleep evades
anorectics as insomnia nestles in. Bodies crave
lovers like sacrifice demand virgins. Everyone becomes
nostalgia. Ancestors beget legends, our bull sitting
amongst flowers. Funerals linger just minutes,
bloody long, and stains trauma-infused hippocampi.
Say you remember. *Sorry,*
so sorry. Saying, *You're nothing, nothing.*
Believe I carry survivors' weight,
immense. An' what shit bulls amass, you
watch. I'll play Ferdinand, see? Blossoms for horns.

Horns for blossoms—see Ferdinand play. I'll watch
you amass bullshit. What an immense
weight survivors carry. I believe
nothing, nothing you're saying. Sorry, so
sorry. *Remember*, you say.
Hippocampi infused trauma stains and long, bloody
minutes just linger. Funeral flowers amongst
Sitting Bull, our legends beget ancestors. Nostalgia
becomes everyone. Virgins demand sacrifice like lovers
crave bodies. In nestles insomnia as anorectics
evade sleep—slumber foregone. Dormant: our
forgotten, lost histories. Our stories are twisted.
Lies upon lies they wrote. We all act red.

Directions for Lazarus drug: let's grip wings and hope.
Release prayers for life (an exchange). Still nothing?
Resurrections aren't privileges. Stalemate. Who's playing god
now? Doctors invented drugs to mimic marvels. Diluted
genius poured and bottled manmade poisons. Now, death's
patient. The count multiplies and heroin begets opioids.
Win or lose, it's: one, resuscitate, two, resuscitate … can you breathe?
Just try. They try, paramedics and lovers. Giving life is power.

Power is life-giving. Lovers and paramedics try, they try. Just
breathe. You can resuscitate two, resuscitate one, it's lose or win.
Opioids beget heroin and multiplies. Count the patient
deaths now. Poisons made man bottled and poor—genius
deluded. Marvels mimic, too. Drugs invented doctors. Now
god's playing who? Stalemate. Privileges aren't resurrections
(nothing, still). Exchange a life for prayers. Release
hope and wings grip. Let's drug Lazarus for directions.

Mind your collapse. Will you practice with god-
therapists the who's who of normality? A, *You're so volatile.*
I'm so disappointed. Your nightmares mean
bedlam. To sacrifice love, my desire, you whisper
demons to me. To me, screaming women
was childhood. Horror was family.
Me watching (Daddy's drunk again). Baby, hey,
baby, hey—saying you're
remembering me is perdition. Now, even,
you're still inside me. You're within
darkness, sudden as bruised bones.

With Practice You Will Collapse Your Mind

Bones bruised as sudden darkness
within—you're me. Inside, still. You're
even now. Perdition is me remembering
your saying, *Hey, baby,*
hey, baby. Again, drunk Daddy's watching me.
Family was horror. Childhood was
women screaming. (Me, too. Me, too). Demons
whisper, *You desire my love? Sacrifice two lamb.* Bed
means nightmares. You're disappointed. So? I'm
volatile. So? You're a normality of who's who. The therapists,
god . . . with practice, you will collapse your mind. .

27

Walls building panic—we're corralled
calves ready for waiting
butchers. We're virtuous nobodies now,
scarred and wounded. Forehead's
bloodied, our fear curdled. Hatred's fed
well—this growing smorgasbord's
run rancid with disease. Spread
lies like pigs' slop. *Animal Farm*,
another ignored prophecy (predictable).
Action dictates character as inaction
molds complacency. Leopards laying
with goats and babies caressing
vipers . . . is this not our America?

America or not, this is vipers
caressing babies and goats with
lying leopards. Complacency molds
inaction as character dictates action.
Predictable—prophecy ignored another
farm animal. Slop pigs like lies
spread disease with rancid-run
smorgasbords growing. This well-
fed hatred's curdled. Fear our bloodied
foreheads, wounded and scarred.
Now nobody's virtuous. We're butchers
waiting for ready calves.
Corralled panic building walls.

Am I that wolf, ravenous and howling?
Midnight shifts pack the darkening,
each with blood-craving and feral
eyes. Together we are powerful; crazy,
how rampage creates fear. Everyone for abattoirs,
there's bolts for brains or teeth for necks.
All nature, it's all nature—
we're predators whose alpha
becomes unsuspecting omega. Fragile
cattle, my prey, remain still. You'll be my
sacrifice. A testament, gimme something—
anything. Gimme oblations or atonement.

Atonement or oblations, gimme anything—
something. Gimme testament, a sacrifice,
maybe. You'll still remain prey. My cattle
fragile, omega unsuspecting becomes
alpha. Whose predators are we?
Natural, it's natural—
necks for teeth or brains for bolts, there's
abattoirs for everyone. Fear creates rampage, how
crazy-powerful are we together? Eyes
feral and craving blood. With each
darkening, the pack shifts midnight.
Howling and ravenous, wolf that I am.

Monsters of bedrooms awakening in stumbles.
Baby, the nightmares mean experience. Infants
screaming for comfort (give milk and washed
diapers). Victim playing, victims blaming—innocence
disappearing with understanding. Mama's afternoon,
every one, full o' drink. Fine, it's fine,
it's history repeating and apples falling close.
Kids having babies, thighs sealed with Daddy
watching. Night after night, nothing's different,
nothing's different. There is truth and there
are lies. Your eyes are closed—
we offered prayers to deaf gods.

God's deaf to prayers offered. We
closed our eyes. Your lies are
there and truth is there. Different nothings,
different nothings, night after night. Watching
Daddy with sealed thighs, babies having kids . . .
close-falling apples and repeating history. (It's
fine, it's fine). Drink a full one every
afternoon. Mama's understanding with disappearing
innocence. Victims blaming, victim playing. Diapers
washed and milk give comfort for screaming
infants. Experience mean nightmares. The baby
stumbles in, awakening bedrooms of monsters.

Deceptions profound! declared
time and again (and again). Children gone
missing, parents gnashing bars—
steal away. Everyone takes privilege,
white as bundled wool. Cross this:
bare deserts. Ravaging rivers. We are dying,
we are asking children for sacrifices. These
are what keening coyotes hear: you don't
own your bodies. You're thinking you're
lucky even, or patriotic. Aren't Americans
stars-spangled enough? Raped babies,
killed women, caged people. Masters
carry sticks for power, resisting mutiny.

Mutiny resisting power, for sticks carry
masters. People caged, women killed,
babies raped. Enough spangled stars . . .
Americans aren't patriotic, or even lucky.
You're thinking your body's your own;
don't you hear coyotes keening? What are
these sacrifices for? Children asking, *Are we
dying? Are we?* Rivers ravaging deserts—
bear this cross: wool bundled as white
privilege takes everyone away. Steel
bars gnashing parents missing
gone children, again and again . . . and *TIME*
declared FOUND: PRO DECEPTIONS.

Memories bespoke become ornaments
hanging heavy. So, it's nostalgia, year after year.
Forget wee hours, the in-laws burning
meats, catastrophes of traditions. To have,
we do rituals and formalities. It's, annually,
struggles and fights. Mom hates that
cousin, the boyfriend's numb in eggnog, aunts yelling—
presents conjured the quiet and, like ghosts,
were we miracles? Were we stories children
loved hard like just knights glistening, and quiet
kingdoms of hope? Still, I hold
tight my fantasy, ridiculous and pure. Here, look:
perfectly roasted beef. Children
playing. Here comes Santa, arms
loaded with presents, a god above reindeer.

Dear, reign above god (a presence with loaded
arms). Santa comes here. Playing
children, beef roasted perfectly . . .
look, here: pure and ridiculous fantasy (my tight
hold). I still hope of kingdoms
quiet and glistening knights just like hard-loved
children's stories. We were miracles, we were
ghost-like, and quiet the conjured presence.
Yelling aunts, eggnog in numb boyfriends, the cousin
that hates Mom. Fights and struggles.
Annually, it's formalities and rituals. Do we
have to? Traditions of catastrophes meet
burning laws. In the hours we forget,
year after year. Nostalgia, it's so heavy. Hanging
ornaments become bespoke memories.

Rose gardens in winter. Year one:
dreaming of lofts in downtown.
Was I coming home? Was it big cities,
the pearl unearthed? An' here's personal
histories, our lovers and failures. My vegan
strippers and elderly queens, the pronunciation's
Willamette, damnit. Witches of rivers
are watching. Stop coming,
we're so full. Still, you're saying
deport all Californians? City of sanctuaries,
wild and green, so brambling
feral. Keeps it weird, how tunnels birth
towers and hospitals mount hills.

Hills mount hospitals and towers
birth tunnels. How weird, it keeps feral—
brambling, so green and wild.
Sanctuaries of city, Californians all deport,
saying, *You're still full. So? We're*
coming. Stop watching our
rivers of witches. Damnit, *Willamette*
pronunciations. The queen's elderly and stripper's
vegan. My failures and lovers, history's
personal. Here's an unearthed pearl. The
city's big. Was it homecoming? I was
downtown in lofts of dreaming.
One year, winter in gardens rose.

Thanksgiving, me just ambling and angry. To go indigenous,
the All must surrender. Spirit, too, demands Colonizer,
Will you? Will you? Will you or won't you? Questions trample
lips and thick accents are unfamiliar. Strangeness is now
everywhere. Masca means witch. Baby witch,
mascotte, charm. Masco becomes mascot. Imagine, you:
all I am, me, untangling everythings. Redskins. Cleveland Indians.
Him, too, stick the snapback on. Land, the giver,
you till. Watch, I'll call on our ancestors, our blood and massacres
were here second. Resilience and strength were first.
Tears through miles with feet bloodied for what?
For what? Remember, miles make radicals.
Didn't you know? No, you didn't. Yet here we are.

Are we here yet? Didn't you know? No, you didn't.
Radicals make miles, remember. What for?
What for? Bloodied feet with miles through tears.
First were strength and resilience. Second here were
massacres and blood. Our ancestors are on call. I'll watch 'til you
give'er the land on back. Snap the stick to him.
Indians cleave land. Skin's red. Everything's untangling me—am I all
you imagine? Mascot becomes masco. Charm, mascotte,
witch baby, witch means masca. Everywhere
now is strangeness. Unfamiliar are accents thick and lips
trample questions. *You won't or you will? You will? You will?*
Colonizer demands two-spirit surrender. Must all the
indigenous go, too? Angry and ambling, just me giving thanks.

Waiting werewolves, we're rabid and wild. Moons direct movements, killing desires—inside, we're animals. The reminder, solemn, a hearsay everyone overlooks. We, enslavement undone, lycan through and through. Abominations were here, in bars and backseats. In here it's feral. Gone, we're becoming. We are what legends nourish. Children tell wee stories and tales tall as boogeymen. See you after morning—the dawn brings awakenings. Howling, heads lifted, are we different now?

Now different, we are lifted heads. Howling
awakenings bring dawn. The morning
after, you see boogeymen as tall
tales and stories we tell children. Nourish
legends. What are we becoming? We're
gone, feral. It's here, in backseats and bars. In
here, we're abominations through and through.
Like an undone enslavement, we look over
everyone. Say here, a solemn reminder, *The animals
we are inside desires killing.* Movement direct
moons. Wild and rabid, we're wolves, we're waiting.

Human remains arrive, that all could
live and love crumble so small. Was Mama
really bones and sand? Oceans, the taste . . .
       water enough for drowning, salt
plentiful for dying. *Turn heads*, Sodom calls,
look—angels' warning ignored. We are curious,
how burning cities are irresistible. Fires meant
cleansing, a second chance. A forefather asked,
I conquer, do I not? Did you watch? You didn't
even hear we're coming. We're silent, shoes
in sand, bodies becoming pillars—dust for dust.

Dust for dust, pillars becoming bodies. Sand in
shoes, silent, we're coming. We're here—even.
Didn't you watch? You did not. I do conquer. I
asked Father for a second chance. A cleansing
meant fires. Irresistible are cities burning. How
curious are we? Ignored warning angels. *Look*,
calls Sodom. Heads turn. Dying for plentiful
sand, drowning for enough water.
Taste the oceans. Sand and bones, really.
(Mama was small). So, crumble love and live.
Could all that arrive remain human?

See the pictures? He, alone, recalls it all. And memory
lingers here. Sick heads make regrets
huge and away swim mistakes like whales.
Sorry, he's human. He's sorry he's scared—
he's Jonah of full bellies. Our broken
system's the offender, another
mishap, another bias. Here's to oceans of dreams.
Lost, he's landlocked. All we're doing,
we are what hatred spawns. Suspicion
means this: forced solitude and life in prisons.
Everyone made deals—
all for views, water painted views.

Views, painted water views for all.
Deals made everyone
prisons in life and solitude forced. This means
suspicion spawns hatred. What are we
doing? We're all landlocked. He's lost
dreams of oceans, too. Here's bias: another mishap,
another offender. The system's
broken . . . our belly's full of Jonah. He's
scared, he's sorry he's human, he's sorry.
Whales like mistakes swim away and huge
regrets make heads sick. Here lingers
memory and all it recalls. Alone, he pictures the sea.

"America d'Colonizer." *Yellow Medicine Review*, May 2020.
"FOUND: PRO DECEPTIONS." *Yellow Medicine Review*, May 2020.
"No Man Struggles." *Yellow Medicine Review*, May 2020.
"Panic Building Walls." *The Social Justice Review*, July 2019.

J.C. (Tyner) Mehta, born and raised in Oregon and a citizen of the Cherokee Nation, is a multi-award-winning interdisciplinary author, artist, and storyteller. She has received several writer-in-residencies around the world which were pivotal in supporting the creation of 15 published books. These posts include the Hosking Houses Trust with an appointment at The Shakespeare Birthplace (Stratford-Upon-Avon, UK), Paris Lit Up (Paris, France), the Women's International Study Center (WISC) Acequia Madre House post (Santa Fe, NM), the Kimmel Harding Nelson Center for the Arts (Nebraska City, NE), and a Writer in the Schools (WITS) residency at Literary Arts (Portland, OR). She is currently the post-graduate research representative at the Centre for Victorian Studies at the University of Exeter, England. She is the first Native American to serve in this role at the largest institutional Victorian research center in Great Britain. Her doctoral research addresses the intersection of eating disorders and poetry. Learn more about Jessica at her website, www.thischerokeerose.com, where you will find links to her books, upcoming projects, and the Emmy award winning documentary on her life and work from Osiyo Television.

New Rivers Press emerged from a drafty Massachusetts barn in winter 1968. Intent on publishing work by new and emerging poets, founder C.W. "Bill" Truesdale labored for weeks over an old Chandler & Price letterpress to publish three hundred fifty copies of Margaret Randall's collection *So Many Rooms Has a House but One Roof.* About four hundred titles later, New Rivers is now a nonprofit learning press, based since 2001 at Minnesota State University Moorhead. Charles Baxter, one of the first authors with New Rivers, calls the press "the hidden backbone of the American literary tradition."

As a learning press, New Rivers guides student editors, designers, writers, and filmmakers through the various processes involved in selecting, editing, designing, publishing, and distributing literary books. in working, learning, and interning with New Rivers Press, students gain integral real-world knowledge that they bring with them into the publishing workforce at positions with publishers across the country, or to begin their own small presses and literary magazines.

Please visit our website: newriverspress.com for more information.